Date: 4/12/11

Snails Are Gross!

Leigh Rockwood

PowerKiDS
press

New York

Published in 2011 by The Rosen Publishing Group, Inc.
29 East 21st Street, New York, NY 10010

First Edition

Editor: Maggie Murphy
Book Design: Ashley Burrell
Photo Researcher: Jessica Gerweck

Photo Credits: Cover, pp. 4, 6, 7, 8, 10, 11, 16, 17, 20, 21, 22 Shutterstock.com; p. 5 © www.iStockphoto.com/Christophe Rolland; p. 9 Eduardo Velasco/Getty Images; p. 12 © Biosphoto/Bringard Denis/Peter Arnold, Inc.; p. 13 (top) © www.iStockphoto.com/Vesna Sajn; p. 13 (bottom left) © www.iStockphoto.com/Urs Renggli; p. 13 (bottom right) © Wendell Metzen/age fotostock; p. 14–15 © www.iStockphoto.com/Wouter van Caspel; p. 18 © FLPA/David Hosking/age fotostock; p. 19 © www.iStockphoto.com/Nuno Lopes.

Library of Congress Cataloging-in-Publication Data

Rockwood, Leigh.
  Snails are gross! / Leigh Rockwood. — 1st ed.
      p. cm. — (Creepy crawlies)
  Includes index.
  ISBN 978-1-4488-0699-7 (library binding) — ISBN 978-1-4488-1359-9 (pbk.) — ISBN 978-1-4488-1360-5 (6-pack)
  1. Snails—Juvenile literature. I. Title.
  QL430.4.R625 2011
  594'.3—dc22
                                        2010006018

Manufactured in the United States of America

CPSIA Compliance Information: Batch #WS10PK: For Further Information contact Rosen Publishing, New York, New York at 1-800-237-9932

Contents

Slow and Creepy

Snails are slimy, slow-moving animals that are found throughout the world. They live in freshwater, in salt water, and on land. A snail's body is basically a foot, a head, and a shell. A snail crawls along by wiggling its foot. As it does this,

Snails are close relatives of slugs.

If you pick up a snail, be sure to wash your hands afterward! Snails can carry germs that could make you sick.

the snail's body makes **mucus** that helps it move. This gross mucus leaves a trail of slime behind the snail wherever it goes!

How slow is a snail? The garden snail is the world's slowest animal. It moves at about .03 mile per hour (.05 km/h). At that speed, it would take a snail more than a day to go the length of a football field!

Slimy Body

The snail belongs to a group of **mollusks** called **gastropods**. Most of its soft, boneless body is made up of a foot. The head is at the front of the body. This is where the snail's mouth and **antennae** are. There are two pairs of antennae. The longer pair has eyespots, which the snail

Here, you can see both sets of this snail's antennae.

A snail's shell forms a spiral.

uses to see. The shorter pair is used for its senses of touch and smell.

A snail's shell helps keeps its body safe. A snail can crawl into its shell when the weather is too hot or too cold. It can also crawl into its shell if it is in danger from an animal that wants to eat it.

This tiny snail is climbing up a blade of grass.

There are thousands of snail **species** in the world. You may have seen snails on the ground. Did you know, though, that there are also snails that live in rivers, lakes, and oceans? Snails that live in water breathe using **gills**. Snails that live on land breathe using simple **lungs**.

Snails, such as this one, that live in the world's seas and oceans are called sea snails.

Snails come in many sizes. The smallest snails are less than .02 inch (.5 mm) long. One of the world's largest snails lives in the seas near Australia and is about 2 feet (61 cm) long. The world's largest land snail is the giant African snail, which can be about 15.5 inches (39 cm) long and weigh about 2 pounds (907 g).

Most land snails live in the soil and among the plants of **habitats** that are not too cool and not too dry. These snails have dull-colored shells. This helps them blend in with their habitats and keep away from **predators** that want to eat them.

This snail is crawling on tree moss. Tree moss grows in wet, shady places, where snails like to live.

Many freshwater snails and land snails live in habitats where frogs also live.

▼

Different species of sea snails live throughout the world's seas and oceans. Most live in **tidal** waters. These are places close to shore that are underwater only at certain times of the day. Freshwater snails live in flowing rivers and streams as well as in the still water of lakes and ponds.

11

Life Cycle

2

Adult snails have both male and female parts. Before the two snails **mate**, they cover each other in slime. Then, each snail **fertilizes** the eggs in its own body with the help of the other snail.

1

Land snails hatch from eggs. When they hatch, the baby snails look like tiny adults. However, unlike adult snails, they have very soft shells. Snails reach adulthood when they are about two years old.

How does a snail make its shell? It has a body part called a mantle. The mantle lets out a liquid. As this liquid dries, it hardens into a shell. As the mantle keeps letting out this liquid, the shell builds up and gets bigger.

Each snail lays about 100 eggs. Generally, the eggs are laid just under the soil. Between two and four weeks later, the eggs hatch.

3

Fact Sheet: GROSS!

1 A newborn snail is hungry. It will eat its own eggshell after it hatches. Sometimes it will even eat its unhatched siblings!

2 People all over the world eat snails. In France, they are cooked in their shells with butter and garlic.

3 Scientists often make up names that tell you something about what an animal looks like. Snails are part of a group of animals called gastropods. That word is Latin for "stomach-foot"!

4 In **tropical** areas, there are snails that live in trees. Their shells are brightly colored and thinner than land snails' shells.

There are skin creams that have snail slime in them. The people who make these creams claim that the slime is good for your skin!

5

Some people keep snails in their fish tanks. The snail helps keep the tank clean by eating the **algae** that builds up on the walls of the tank.

6

The garden snail was brought to the United States in the 1800s. Since that time, it has become a pest to gardeners because the garden snail eats the garden's plants.

7

In 2007, Alastair Galpin of New Zealand let 8 snails sit on his face. This set a world record. In 2009, Fin Keleher of Utah broke that record by letting 43 snails sit on his face!

8

Snacking Snails

Land snails eat mostly rotting plants. Gross! They also eat living plants and tree bark. Freshwater snails eat rotting plants as well as algae. Some species also eat dead animals that are in the water. Most sea snails eat algae. A few species of snails hunt and kill other animals for food. The whelk is a sea snail that eats

This snail is snacking on some grass.

People keep some kinds of snails as pets. This pet snail is eating a piece of celery.

clams. The whelk grabs the clam in its foot. Then, it forces the clam's shell open and eats the clam.

A snail eats its food using its radula. The radula is a tonguelike body part that has tiny toothlike parts, called denticles. As the denticles wear down, new ones take their places.

Giant African Snails

Giant African snails are land snails that live in eastern Africa. They can be as large as 15.5 inches (39 cm) long and weigh 2 pounds (907 g), but most are about half that size. These snails eat almost any plant they see. They also eat small rocks and the paint on the outsides of houses!

Here, a giant African snail in Madagascar is shown. Madagascar is an island country off the southeastern coast of Africa.

Giant African snails can lay up to 1,200 eggs each year.

▼

It is against the law in the United States to have giant African snails as pets. They can carry germs that make people sick. There is another problem with these snails, too. If they are put into the wild in habitats where they do not belong, they can hurt the plants in that habitat. This can then have an effect on the animals in that habitat.

That's What Shells Are For!

Snails are much too slow to run away from their predators. When they are in danger, they do the next best thing. They curl up in their shells to keep themselves safe. Some snails use their feet to close off the shell's opening. Other

Here, a snail curls up in its shell.

Snails seal themselves in their shells with their own mucus during estivation.

snails use their slime to seal themselves in.

Snails also close themselves inside their shells when the weather is too hot or too dry. The snail's body then goes into a slowed-down state, called **estivation**. During a period of estivation, a snail will not need much food or water. It can stay like this for days, weeks, or even months.

Snails have many predators, such as bugs, birds, frogs, fish, snakes, and even people! However, the fact that many animals eat snails makes them an important part of the **food chains** to which they belong.

A food chain is what links all the animals in a habitat to each other. Snails are near the bottom of the food chains to which they belong.

Now that you know more about snails, you can try to find them where you live. If you find a snail's shell, you will know how the snail made it. If you see a trail of mucus, there might just be a slimy snail nearby!

Glossary

algae (AL-jee) Plantlike living things without roots or stems that live in water.

antennae (an-TEH-nee) Thin, rodlike feelers on the heads of certain animals.

estivation (es-teh-VAY-shun) A state in which body systems slow down when it is too hot or dry.

fertilizes (FUR-tuh-lyz-ez) Puts male cells inside an egg to make babies.

food chains (FOOD CHAYNZ) Groups of living things that are each other's food.

gastropods (GAS-truh-podz) Kinds of soft-bellied mollusks that have heads and one foot.

gills (GILZ) Body parts that fish and other animals use for breathing.

habitats (HA-beh-tats) The kinds of land where an animal or a plant naturally lives.

lungs (LUNGZ) The parts of an air-breathing animal that take in air and supply oxygen to the blood.

mate (MAYT) To come together to make babies.

mollusks (MAH-lusks) Animals without backbones and with soft bodies and, often, shells.

mucus (MYOO-kus) Thick, slimy matter produced by the bodies of many animals.

predators (PREH-duh-terz) Animals that kill other animals for food.

species (SPEE-sheez) One kind of living thing. All people are one species.

tidal (TY-dul) Having to do with the daily rise and fall of the ocean.

tropical (TRAH-puh-kul) Warm year-round.

Index

A
algae, 15–16

B
body, 4–7, 12, 21

E
eggs, 12–13

F
foot, 4, 6, 17

G
gastropods, 6, 14
gills, 8
group, 6, 14

H
habitat(s), 10, 19
head, 4, 6

L
land, 4, 8
lungs, 8

M
mollusks, 6
mouth, 6
mucus, 5, 22

P
predators, 10, 20, 22

S
senses, 6
shell(s), 4, 7, 10, 12, 14, 17, 20–22
slime, 5, 12, 15, 21
species, 8, 11, 16

T
trail, 5, 22
trees, 14

W
water(s), 4, 8, 11, 16, 21
weather, 7, 21

Web Sites

Due to the changing nature of Internet links, PowerKids Press has developed an online list of Web sites related to the subject of this book. This site is updated regularly. Please use this link to access the list: www.powerkidslinks.com/creep/snail/